Gospel of Mark
Simplified Cowboy Version

Kevin Weatherby

Copyright © 2017 Kevin Weatherby

All rights reserved.

ISBN-10: 1542507855
ISBN-13: 978-1542507851

DEDICATION

This book goes out to Ty Weber. You have fed, watered, doctored, and taken care of nearly everything on the ranch while I fulfill what God has called me to do. Your wages have been small, but your reward in heaven will be huge.

You'd be durn near perfect...
...if you were from Texas.

Table of Contents

Chapter 1 ...... *1*
Chapter 2 ...... *6*
Chapter 3 ...... *9*
Chapter 4 ...... *12*
Chapter 5 ...... *16*
Chapter 6 ...... *20*
Chapter 7 ...... *26*
Chapter 8 ...... *30*
Chapter 9 ...... *35*
Chapter 10 ...... *41*
Chapter 11 ...... *47*
Chapter 12 ...... *51*
Chapter 13 ...... *57*
Chapter 14 ...... *61*
Chapter 15 ...... *70*
Chapter 16 ...... *75*

Chapter 1

This ain't about nothing except the Good News of a man named Jesus, the Son of God. ²I reckon it all started when one of God's top hands, a fella named Isaiah, wrote this:

"God said, 'I got a cowboy coming that is going to show you a new message and a new way of riding for me. ³He's already shouting from the desert and tellin' y'all to get ready to saddle up for the Lord and ride right straight for him.'"

⁴So John came out of nowhere riding for God and baptizing folks. His message was a plain and simple, "Quit riding in sin and be baptized and God will turn a blind eye to all the sorry things you've done." ⁵Folks came from all around the country to hear this cowboy preach. Many a heart turned to God and they told of the sorry things they had done and old John dunked 'em in Jordan Creek.

⁶John was a different sort of fellow. He wore a vest of camel hair with a stout leather belt holding his jeans up. He didn't waste no time with fancy vittles, but just ate locusts and wild honey. ⁷He told people time and again, "The Top Hand is coming soon and I ain't worthy enough to pull his boots off after a long ride. ⁸I dunk y'all in water, but he's gonna dunk you in the Holy Spirit."

⁹It wasn't long before Jesus came riding down from the

Nazareth country and told John to baptize him in Jordan Creek. ¹⁰When Jesus came up out of the water, the sky split plum apart and you could see right into heaven. And out of heaven come the Spirit of God like a dove and it came right down to him. ¹¹Then there was a voice from heaven that said, "You are my boy and that pleases me to no end." ¹²Then the Spirit of God led Jesus out into the wilds and the brush where there were no fences and things were hard to come by. Jesus was out there for more'n forty days with nothing to eat and satan tried to take him out time and again. Jesus spent all those nights surrounded by all sorts of predators, but God sent angels to take care of him.

¹⁴After all this, old John was thrown in jail and Jesus went into the Galilee country to tell people the Good News. ¹⁵He told 'em, "Y'all been waiting for a long time and the Boss' Green Pasture has made it here. Quit riding in sin and tie hard and fast to the Good News." ¹⁶As Jesus rode along telling people this same message over and over, he run into a couple of fellows near the Sea of Galilee. These two cowboys, Simon and Andrew, were gathering some heifers. ¹⁷Jesus hollered over to 'em and said, "Ride with me and I'll teach you how to gather cowboys." ¹⁸They immediately coiled their ropes up and loped off after him. ¹⁹As they were riding, they came upon a cowboy named James and his brother John. ²⁰They were patching a water trough and Jesus told 'em to saddle up and ride with him. James and John left their old dad sitting there as they rode off with Jesus.

[21]The cowboys rode all the way to Capernaum. When the Day of Rest came (the old timers called it the Sabbath), Jesus went up to the church building and began to give all them folks a clinic on what it means to ride for God. [22]These folks couldn't believe what he was teaching them. It was like he knew what he was talking about instead of being like those other preachers that just wanted to hear themselves talk and make up rules. [23]Just then, a fellow that had an evil way about him shouted out, [24]"You leave us alone Jesus! Have you come here to wipe us out? I know who you really are—God's Top Hand!" [25]But Jesus shushed him with a look and without raising his voice he said, "Be quiet and come out." [26]That fellow fell down like he'd been hit with a whiskey bottle and the evil spirit that had a hold of the him yelped like a whipped pup as it came out of the man. [27]People stood there with their mouths hanging wide open and they turned to each other and said, "Did you see that? This cowboy is teaching us something new. He not only knows what he's doing, but even the evil spirits jump when he says to." [28]Word spread quickly in the country around Galilee about this new cowboy with a new way. [29]When they left the church, they rode over to Simon and Andrew's line camp. James and John were still with them and as they all walked in, [30]it was apparent that Simon's mother-in-law had something bad sick about her. They were asking Jesus what should be done when [31]he just pushed passed them and took her by the hand and helped her stand up. By the time she reached her feet, she was as right as spring rain. She felt so good she

Gospel of Mark **3**

went in and fried up some frijoles and tortillas.

³²⁻³³That evening, people started coming by the line camp and asking Jesus to fix all those people who had an evil way about them or those who were feeling mighty poorly. ³⁴Jesus fixed ever' single one of 'em. He didn't let any of the demons open their mouths because they knew who he was and Jesus wasn't ready for everyone to know just yet.

³⁵The next morning, Jesus was saddled up way before daylight. He rode a far piece out into the pasture to be alone and pray. ³⁶Simon and the other cowboys looked and looked for him. ³⁷When they finally found him, they said, "Everyone is scouring the country for you." ³⁸Jesus swung up in the saddle and said, "Let's make a big circle into the surrounding country so I can tell people the Good News. That's why my Dad sent me." ³⁹So Jesus and his Cowboys rode all through Galilee where Jesus gave clinics in the churches and cast out many a demon along the way.

⁴⁰A man with rotting skin came to Jesus and fell down in front of him, asking him for help. "If you had a mind to, I know you could fix me, Jesus." ⁴¹Jesus was touched by this man's way of asking and he felt sorry for him. Jesus reached out to the man and touched him, saying, "I am of a mind—be fixed!" ⁴²The rotting skin immediately fell off him and he was clean. ⁴³But Jesus gave him a stern warning before he let him go, ⁴⁴"Don't tell anyone what happened here. Just go to the church and show 'em that you're clean. Take along the

offering that Moses said to bring for your fixing." ⁴⁵But that fellow couldn't keep quiet about the great thing that Jesus had done for him. Word spread around so quickly that Jesus couldn't even come into town because of the mobs of people that came to him. Because of this, he camped way out where it was hard to find him, but people still came to find him from all parts of the region.

Chapter 2

A few days later, Jesus rode back to Capernaum and news spread quickly that he was back in the home country. ²So many people gathered at the house Jesus was at that there was no longer any room to stand, not even by the door. But Jesus preached the Good News to all that were there and could hear him. ³Some people brought a paralyzed fellow to see him, but they couldn't even get in the house. ⁴These guys were so adamant about getting their friend to Jesus that they climbed up on the roof and dug out the section right above where he was talking. They lowered their friend on a stretcher right down in front of him. Jesus smiled and admired their boldness and their faith. ⁵He said to the paralyzed man, "Your sins have been forgotten." ⁶There were some religious experts watching and they were all thinking, ⁷"Who does this cowboy think he is? Only God can forgive sins." ⁸Quick as a cow kick, Jesus knew exactly what these so called "religious experts" were thinking. He decided to clear the air. He asked them, "Why are your thoughts so screwed up with what I just did? ⁹Is it easier to say that a man's sins are forgotten or is it easier to tell him to get up and walk? ¹⁰But just so you know that God's Top Hand has the authority on earth to forget sins…" He turned to the paralyzed man and said, ¹¹"Stand up cowboy. Take your bedroll and go home." ¹²Immediately the paralyzed man stood up and did as he was told. He walked out of the house in front of them all. Everyone was slack jawed. They started saying, "We've never seen anything like this!"

¹³Jesus rode out again along the area close by the sea. A whole crowd came with him and he gave them a clinic on how to ride for God's outfit. ¹⁴As they continued on their travels to spread the Good News, he saw a fellow named Levi sitting in a tax collector's booth. "Saddle up, cowboy," he said to him. Levi left everything right there and rode off with them. ¹⁵They rode over to Levi's place to have some grub and a lot of Levi's friends were there. These fellows were all tax collectors, outcasts, and outlaws. ¹⁶When the religious experts and bigwig preachers saw who Jesus was eating with, they asked his cowboys, "Why does he eat with such low-life? ¹⁷When Jesus heard their question, he said to them. "Those that are healthy don't need to be doctored, but those that are sick do. I have not come to gather the old pet cows, but the outcasts and outlaws with nines in their tails."

¹⁸There was this one time that the guys that rode with John the Baptist, as well as some other goody-goody preachers, were going without food for religious reasons. All these folks came to Jesus and asked, "Why do all those that follow John, and those that follow the Pharisees, go without food in order to get closer to God, but your cowboys don't?" ¹⁹Jesus smiled a wry smile and said, "If a cowboy invites his buddies over for a BBQ, he doesn't expect them to go hungry does he? Of course not. As long as the cowboy is cooking,

Gospel of Mark 7

his guests will be eating. [20]There will come a time when the cowboy will no longer be around and that is when they will fast. [21]Besides, you don't put a new patch on old wranglers. If you do, you'll end up with a bigger tear than when you started. [22]Also, you can't put new hooch in an old wineskin. If you do, the new hooch will expand and bust the wineskin open. New wine is poured in new wineskin."

[23]A little while after that, Jesus and his cowboys were riding through some grain fields on the Day of Rest. They got hungry and picked some heads of wheat for a quick snack. [24]Some of those bigwig preachers saw this and accused them of violating the Sacred Day of Rest. [25]Jesus replied calmly, "Didn't you read where David and his cowboyss got hungry and went in and [26]ate the special bread. You all know that is against the law for anyone to eat except the priests?" [27]Then he told them, "The Day of Rest was made for cowboys. Cowboys were not made for the Day of Rest. God's Top Hand is Boss-even of the Day of Rest."

Chapter 3

Another time, Jesus walked into a church and there was a fellow there with a crippled wing. ²The bigwig preachers kept an eye on Jesus to see if he would heal the guy on the Day of Rest. They were always on the lookout for some way to talk bad about him. ³Jesus said to the guy, "Come up front for a second." ⁴Then Jesus turned to all the scowling preachers and said, "Is it against the Law to do something good for someone who is in a bad way?" They sat there and didn't say a word. ⁵Jesus looked hard at them, but he felt sorry for 'em because of their stubbornness and pride. He told the guy with the crippled wing, "Stretch out your hand." He stretched it out and it was completely normal. ⁶Them bigwig preachers went straight out and began planning how they could kill Jesus.

⁷Then Jesus rode back out towards the Sea of Galilee and a ton of people ⁸followed after him because of the great things he was doing. ⁹There were so many people, he told his cowboys to stack some hay up so the crowd wouldn't mash him. ¹⁰He had healed so many people with various ailments that all kinds of sick people were trying to touch him. ¹¹But whenever a demon saw him, they would always fall down and holler out, "You are the Son of God: His Top Hand!" ¹²But Jesus always kept the demons from telling anyone who he really was.

Gospel of Mark

¹³Now Jesus rode up onto the mountain and asked some guys to ride with him. ¹⁴He chose twelve cowboys to ride with him so he could teach them his ways and they could show others. He also gave them the power to ¹⁵whip demons that were hurting people. ¹⁶These are the names of Jesus' twelve cowboys: Simon, who Jesus gave the name of Pete; ¹⁷to the brothers James and John, he called them the Sons of Thunder; and the rest were called ¹⁸Andy, Phil, Bart, Matt, Tom, the other James, Thad, Simon the Fanatic, ¹⁹and Judas, who would double-cross Jesus.

²⁰Jesus rode back home and there was so many people needing him that there wasn't even time enough to grab a sandwich. ²¹When his family heard what was happening, they tried to go get him. They thought he was going crazy. ²²The religious experts came all the way from Jerusalem, but they said he was possessed by the devil and that is how he was able to cast out the demons. ²³So Jesus called them all around and told them stories: "How can the devil cast out the devil? ²⁴A cowboy divided against himself ropes no cattle. ²⁵A person against himself has come to his end. ²⁷But no one can steal a ranch's cattle unless he first ties up the cowboy watching over it. Then they can rustle anything they find. ²⁸I'm telling you straight, every wrong can be forgiven, ²⁹but anyone who rejects the love of God and attributes the Holy Spirit's work to the devil, that person's sin will not be forgiven." ³⁰He said all this because they were accusing him of being possessed by a demon.

³¹While all this was happening, Jesus' mom and brothers finally found him. They were standing outside the house where he was and ³²they sent some people in to get him. Someone in the crowd said, "Hey! Your mom and brothers are outside looking for you." ³³He shrugged and said, "Who is my mom and who are my brothers?" ³⁴He motioned towards all the cowboys that were sitting around and learning from him. "Here is my family right here. Whoever rides for the Boss' outfit is my family."

Chapter 4

One day Jesus rode down to the lake. There was such a large crowd that he jumped up on a stack of hay. ²He taught them a lot of things by telling them stories. He said, ³"A farmer went out to plant his fields. ⁴As he planted, some of the seed fell on the road, and the birds ate it all up. ⁵Other seeds fell next to some rocks where there wasn't much dirt. The seeds took root quickly in the shallow soil, ⁶but they withered quickly because there was nowhere for the roots to go. ⁷Other seeds fell among the cactus and thistles. They sprouted, but were choked out by the thorns. ⁸And finally, some seeds found good soil and produced a lot of grain. Some of it yielded thirty times as much, some sixty, and still some a hundred times. ⁹Whoever has ears should be listening."

¹⁰Later on, when they were alone, some of his cowboys asked about the stories. ¹¹He told them, "The secret of the Boss' Outfit has been given to you. But for the sake of everyone else, I teach with stories ¹²so this old saying would come true:

> They look, but cannot see. They hear, but they cannot understand. If they could see and understand, they would turn to me and be forgiven.

¹³Then Jesus said, "If you can't understand this simple

story about the seeds, how are you going to understand all the other stories? ¹⁴The farmer spreads God's Good News to others. ¹⁵The seed that fell on the road stands for those that hear the Good News, but they let satan take it away before it does anything to them. ¹⁶The seed in the rocks stands for those who love the Good News and immediately act like it changes their whole world. ¹⁷But they don't last long because it was all emotion and no faith. They wither quickly when faced with any kind of adversity. ¹⁸The seed that fell among the thorns stands for those who hear God's Good News, ¹⁹but the words that could save them are choked out by worry, lusting after money, and the desire for materialistic things. ²⁰And finally, the seed that found good ground are those people that hear the Good News and do something with it. They produce a harvest of thirty, sixty, or even a hundred times as much as has been planted."

²¹Then Jesus posed a question to them, "Would you light a lamp and then stick it in your bedroll? Of course not. A lamp is lifted up high so that its light can shine far. ²²Everything in the dark will eventually be revealed. ²³If you got ears, you'd best use them for listening to what I'm saying."

²⁴Then he added, "Don't let what I'm saying go in one ear and out the other. The closer you listen the more you'll start getting—and when you start getting it, you'll be given even more. ²⁵To those who listen and apply what I say to do, they'll start catching on even more and more. But if you

Gospel of Mark **13**

ignore the things I say, you'll end up losing more than you started with."

²⁶Jesus also told them, "God's Green Pasture is like a farmer that plants seeds in a field. ²⁷Whether he is asleep at night or working a horse in the arena, those seeds are starting to grow. ²⁸He has no idea how it works, but he knows it does. The earth makes things grow. First a little green leaf pokes up through the dirt. Then the head of wheat forms. ²⁹And finally, the grain is ready for harvest. Then the farmer comes and cuts the wheat with a sickle.

³⁰Jesus said, "How can I tell you about the Boss' Outfit? What kind of cowboy tale will help you understand? ³¹It is like a tiny little mustard seed. It may start out tiny, ³²but it grows to be the biggest plant in the garden. It grows large and ends up providing shade and protection."

³³Jesus used a lot of stories like these in his clinics. ³⁴Truth be told, he never gave a public clinic without using stories, but later when it was just him and his cowboys, he'd explain everything to them.

³⁵When the sun finally set that day, Jesus told his cowboys, "Let's get our tack and cross the lake to the other side." ³⁶So they found a boat, leaving all the crowds behind. ³⁷But soon, after they had bedded down for the night, a terrible storm came upon them. Lightning struck all around and the wind threatened to blow them all away…if the waves didn't drown

them first. ³⁸Jesus was sleeping in his bedroll with his head on his saddle. The cowboys woke him up, yelling, "Boss, don't you care that this storm is going to kill us all?"

³⁹Jesus lifted up on one elbow and said to the storm, "Cut it out and be still!" The winds immediately stopped and all the clouds disappeared. It was as calm as if nothing had ever happened. ⁴⁰After a second he said, "Why are y'all so scared? Don't you have faith in me?"

⁴¹The cowboys looked at each other with wide eyes. "Who are we riding with? Even the wind and lightning gives to his hand."

Chapter 5

The next day, they arrived on the other side of the lake. ²They had no more than got both feet on the ground when a man possessed by an evil spirit started trotting out of the cemetery toward them. ³He lived among the tombs and couldn't even be tied up with chains. ⁴When he was put in irons, he snapped them like paper. No one was strong enough to subdue him. ⁵Night and day he wandered among the dead, howling and caterwauling, and cutting himself with sharp rocks.

⁶Jesus was still a far piece out when the man had caught sight of him. He ran out and bowed real low in front of Jesus. ⁷With an unearthly shriek, he yelled, "Why have you come to stop me, Son of God? By God's Good Name, please don't torture me." ⁸Jesus had already told the spirit to light out.

⁹Jesus said, "What do they call you?"

¹⁰"They call me Legion. We are too many to count." ¹¹He then begged Jesus not to send him away. ¹²There was a herd of pigs grazing nearby and the demonic spirits asked to be sent into the pigs. ¹³Jesus told them to go ahead. The evil spirits rushed out and filled the pigs. Then the herd of two thousand pigs stampeded into the lake and drown.

¹⁴Now the people that had been taking care of that herd

of pigs ran off to tell everyone what had happened. ¹⁵People came running and the first thing they saw was Jesus sitting there talking to the man who had been possessed, but this time he was in his right mind. ¹⁶Word spread quickly about what happened and the people were afraid. They ¹⁷begged Jesus to leave the area.

¹⁸As Jesus threw his saddle back in the boat, the former demon-possessed man asked to ride with him, ¹⁹but Jesus told him to go home. "Tell people what God has done for you and that he had mercy on you." ²⁰So the guy went off and told everyone his story...and all who heard it were amazed.

²¹When Jesus made it back across the lake, a ton of people gathered around him. ²²All of a sudden, one of the local church leaders named Jairus came up, and when he caught sight of Jesus, he fell at his feet. ²³He pleaded with Jesus, "My daughter is near dead. Come and put your hand on her so that she will live." ²⁴Jesus told him to lead the way and a large crowd followed.

²⁵There was also a woman in the crowd that had been bleeding for twelve years. ²⁶She had suffered a great deal and spent everything she had on people that claimed to have a cure. Yet instead of getting better, everything just made her worse. ²⁷She'd heard about Jesus and got close enough to touch his vest. She kept telling herself, ²⁸"I bet if I just touch his clothes, I will be fixed." ²⁹When she touched his vest, her

bleeding immediately stopped and she knew that she'd been healed.

³⁰Jesus also knew that healing power had gone out from him. He turned around and asked, "Who touched me?" ³¹His cowboys kind of chuckled and said, "There's a thousand people within three feet of you and you want to ask, 'Who touched me?'"

³²But Jesus ignored their jibe and continued to look for whoever had laid a hand on him. ³³Then the woman came forward, afraid and shaking like a leaf. She fell down on her face before him and explained what, and why, she'd touched him. ³⁴He said to her, "My daughter, your faith has fixed you. Ride out in peace and be healed."

³⁵While he was still talking to the woman, some people came from the church leader's house saying, "Jairus, your daughter is dead. No need to bother Jesus anymore."

³⁶But Jesus didn't pay no mind to what they people were saying. He told Jairus, "Don't be scared...believe!"

³⁷Jesus didn't let anyone go with him except Pete, James, and John. ³⁸As they neared Jairus' house, there was a terrible commotion of wailing and sobbing coming from inside and out. ³⁹When he went in, he asked why everyone was carrying on like that. Jesus told them that she wasn't dead. The girl was just asleep.

⁴⁰They began making fun of him so he put them all out on the porch. He went into the girl's room with her mom and dad, as well as the three cowboys who'd come with him. ⁴¹Jesus gently took the girl by the hand and said, "Get up, sweetie."

⁴²The twelve year old little girl got up immediately and began to walk around the room like nothing had happened. Everyone was flabbergasted. ⁴³Jesus told 'em all to keep their traps shut about what had happened. If they wanted to do something, they could get the young girl something to eat.

Chapter 6

After all those great things were done, Jesus struck a long trot back to his hometown and his cowboys followed him. ²When the Day of Rest came, Jesus went and did a little preaching at the local church. People who listened were wondering where he came up with all these different interpretations of God's Word. They also wondered where all his wisdom came from and if the miracles he had been performing came from the same place. They all shook their heads and kept asking one another, ³"Isn't this that carpenter? Isn't this Mary's son? Aren't those his sisters that live near here?" Because of all their questions, they didn't hear him; because of their looking for answers elsewhere they couldn't see him; and they got offended that this ordinary fellow would stand up in front and dare to teach them. ⁴Then Jesus said to 'em all, "A cowboy that rides for God gets respect for what he does everywhere except his hometown. All thw people he grew up with, including his family, think they know who he really is, but they don't."

⁵Jesus didn't do any miracles there, except to put his hands on a few sick people and heal them. ⁶He was amazed at how blind all these people that he knew so well were. He stayed around that part of the country though and taught among the ranches and cow towns.

⁷One day, Jesus called his cowboys together and sent them

out to gather people for his Father's brand two by two. ⁸He gave them authority over evil spirits and told them to take nothing along on their journey except their saddles. They couldn't fill their saddlebags with money nor morsels of any kind. ⁹They couldn't even take an extra blue-jean jacket.

¹⁰He told 'em, "When you get to a ranch, stay at their headquarters until you leave that part of the country. ¹¹If a ranch won't welcome you or listen to the Good News, leave that ranch and shake the dust from that place off your boots. That way you will not take any part of an unbelieving outfit with you when you ride off.

¹²So the cowboys set off in pairs to spread the Good News and gather people for God's outfit. They told everyone to turn from their wicked ways and start riding for God. ¹³They cast out many demons that were hurting people and put a little dab of oil on people's heads to show that they ride for God. Many folks were healed.

¹⁴During this, King Herod heard about everything that Jesus was doing. Some were telling him that John the Baptist had been raised from the dead to do miracles ¹⁵and others said that Jesus was Elijah or a new cowboy of God like there used to be in the olden days. ¹⁶But when Herod heard all the rumors he said, "I cut off John the Baptist's head and now he has come back!" ¹⁷Herod was quite a fright because he had had John arrested and killed because he'd made a promise to his wife. That old gal was a burr under his saddle blanket

Gospel of Mark **21**

because she made him kill John. ¹⁸John had criticized Herod for marrying her in the first place. This wasn't just some gal off the street. She had been married to Herod's brother, Philip. It was against God's law to marry your brother's wife if he was still alive and Philip was still kicking around somewhere.

¹⁹So Herodias (Herod's no-account wife) held a grudge against John and wanted to kill him, ²⁰but Herod had kind of taken a liking to a cowboy like John that spoke the truth and rode for God. He didn't really know what to think about the things that John said, but he liked listening to him.

²¹So on Herod's birthday, he threw himself a party and all the important people in his kingdom came to it. ²²⁻²³Herodias' daughter came in and danced for the king. He took such a liking to it that he slipped up and said that she could have anything she wanted—even up to half of his kingdom! ²⁴⁻²⁵She went to her mother and asked her what she should request and her mother said, "The head of John the Baptist on a big ol' plate."

²⁶This shook the king up something fierce, but he'd made a promise in front of a lot of people so he kept it. ²⁷He sent the executioner to the dungeon in which John was being held and the fellow ²⁸came back with John's head and presented it to the king's daughter. She took it straight to her mom. ²⁹When the cowboys who rode alongside John heard that he had been killed, they came and got his body and

buried it with the respect he deserved.

³⁰When all the cowboys got back from their first big gathering for God, they all sat around and told Jesus their stories. ³¹He told 'em, "Let's go somewhere private so we can all talk and rest up." There were tons of people hanging around and wanting to hear everything that Jesus and his cowboys were saying; so much so that they hadn't even had a chance to get a bite to eat.

³²So Jesus and his boys saddled up and headed out, ³³but many saw where they were going and followed them. ³⁴When Jesus saw that there were so many people wanting to know about riding for God, he felt sorry for them. They were like a stray herd looking for water so Jesus taught them many things. In other words, he watered them. Jesus spent a long time teaching and it got to be very late.

³⁵⁻³⁶Some of his cowboys came up and told Jesus to send everyone back to town to eat. ³⁷But he told them, "Y'all get 'em something to eat."

They said, "You want us to ride to town and get all these people something to eat?"

³⁸Jesus responded, "How many loaves of bread do you have already?"

They went and checked their saddle bags and came back and said, "We've got five loaves of bread and a couple of pieces of fish."

³⁹⁻⁴⁰Jesus told his cowboys to sit everyone down in groups of fifty and up to one hundred. While this was being done, ⁴¹Jesus took the five loaves and two pieces of fish, looked up to God and gave thanks, and broke the bread. He gave the pieces of bread and fish to his cowboys to pass out to the hungry crowd. ⁴²There was enough for everybody and no one went away hungry. ⁴³There was even some for leftovers the next day. ⁴⁴Jesus fed over five thousand men, not counting all the women and children that were there too.

⁴⁵Just as soon as they were done, Jesus told his cowboys to get into a nearby boat and go across the sea to Bethsaida. Jesus said goodbye to his boys as the crowd filed away and ⁴⁶then he went up on a nearby mountain to pray and talk to his Dad.

⁴⁷Later that evening, a storm caught the cowboys while in their boat. ⁴⁸Jesus could see his boys straining against the oars as they fought the tumbling sea. When the night was nearly over, he decided to go to Bethsaida and beat them there by walking across the sea as if it were a dry patch of ground. As he was passing them by, ⁴⁹they saw him and got scared out of their skin. ⁵⁰They thought he was some sort of ghost and were terrified. But at the height of their fear, he spoke to them and said, "Don't be scared, boys! It's just me." ⁵¹Then he walked over and climbed into the boat with 'em. When he did, the storm completely stopped. The cowboys

couldn't believe what they had just seen. ⁵²Unfortunately, their hearts were hard because they had already forgot about the loaves and the fish earlier in the day.

⁵³They anchored the boat when they finally got across, and as they came ashore, ⁵⁴people already started recognizing who they all were. ⁵⁶The people ran and told everyone around. Sick people started showing up to be healed. Wherever Jesus and his cowboys went it was like this. People asked if they could just touch his vest, and all that touched him were healed.

Chapter 7

Now some of the head honchos of the church, and some religious experts who were from Jerusalem, gathered around Jesus. ²They saw that some of the cowboys were eating before they had washed their hands ³⁻⁴(it was a religious rule they had made up). ⁵All these uppity-religious fellows asked him, "Why aren't your cowboys keeping the sacred traditions of old. They are eating without washing their hands?"

⁶Jesus calmly replied, "Isaiah foretold the future about you when he said:

'These people will say that they ride for me, but it's just all talk. ⁷What they call church is just teaching a bunch of rules and stuff that they came up with. It's not about me.'

⁸Y'all don't ride for God. You just make up stuff and say it came from Him."

⁹Jesus kept it up and said, "Y'all conveniently shun the commands from God in order to make up your own sorry rules. ¹⁰Even the great cowboy, Moses, said, 'Respect your mom and dad,' and, 'Whoever insults his mom or dad must be killed.' ¹¹But you all tell people that they can get away from helping their parents if they ¹²just say that the money or food is a gift to God. ¹³You teach people to disobey God's command of honoring your mother and father in the name

of greed and tradition. But y'all sure enough don't stop there."

[14] Then Jesus turned away from the religious people and hollered out to the crowd around them, "Listen to me, all of you! [15] What goes in a person don't make him wrong. It's what comes out of him that does."

[17] Jesus rode off and after a long trot, he got to the house he and the cowboys were staying at. As they settled in, some of the cowboys asked him what he meant by his little story about what makes a man wrong in God's eyes. [18] He asked them, "Are y'all that ignorant? Don't you understand that what goes into a person doesn't defile him? [19] Whatever goes into a man goes into his stomach, not his heart. And what goes in the stomach, will end up at the bottom of the outhouse eventually. [20] What comes out of a man's heart is what defiles him. [21] From the heart comes evil desires, all sorts of gross sexual ideas, theft, killing, cheating on your spouse, [22] greed, deceit, perversion, envy, talking bad about others, gossip, pride, and utter foolishness. [23] All these evil things don't come from the outside, they come from a person's heart. That is what defiles them."

[24] After Jesus finished everything he was going to do there, he rode off toward the country around Tyre. He tried to keep his presence there a secret, but that was to no avail. [25] A particular woman who had a daughter that was possessed, heart Jesus had come to town and she went and fell at his

feet. ²⁶This lady wasn't a Jew, but a Greek. She asked Jesus to grab the demon and jerk it out of her daughter. ²⁷Jesus said to her, "A father will feed his own children first. He won't take away their meal and give it to the dogs."

²⁸She answered, "Yes, my Lord, but even the dogs eat the scraps and crumbs that fall from the father's table."

²⁹Jesus smiled at that and said, "That's the kind of faith I'm looking for. You go check on your daughter and see that she has been freed from that scoundrel that's been controlling her."

³⁰When the lady got home, it was just as he'd said. The demon was gone.

³¹Jesus saddled up again and rode away from the country around Tyre and headed through the area of Sidon on his way to the Sea of Galilee. ³²Some fellows found him and brought along a guy who was deaf and couldn't speak. They asked Jesus to put his hands on him and heal him.

³³Jesus took him off to the side and put his fingers in the man's ears. Then he spit on his own fingers and touched the mute man's tongue. ³⁴Jesus looked up to heaven and said quietly, "Open 'em up."

³⁵Immediately, the man's ears were opened and his tongue was loosened. ³⁶Jesus asked everyone around not to say anything about this to anyone, but the more he told 'em to keep

quiet, the more they told everyone of the great things that he was doing. ³⁷They went around saying, "He ain't no counterfeit. He even make the deaf hear and the mute speak."

Chapter 8

For at least the second time, there was another large crowd that had gathered for one of Jesus' clinics. ²Jesus called all his cowboys over to him and said, "I feel sorry for all these people here. They've been here with us for three days and most of them haven't even eaten. ³Some of 'em are so weak they wouldn't even make it home before they fell out."

⁴A few of his cowboys asked, "Where could we find enough tortillas in this desolate country to feed everyone?"

⁵Jesus answered 'em, "How many tortillas do y'all have?"

"Seven," they counted.

⁶Jesus told everyone to take a seat. He took the seven tortillas and tore 'em in half as he gave thanks. He began handing the pieces to the cowboys so they could pass 'em out. ⁷They also had a few pieces of beef jerky. After giving thanks for these, too, he told the cowboys to pass them out as well. ⁸Everyone that was there had plenty of tortillas and enough beef jerky to satisfy the lot of 'em. ⁹There were four thousand people and that was just counting the men.

Jesus immediately sent everyone home and with his cowboys, ¹⁰they struck out at a long trot for the area around Dalmanutha.

¹¹When he got where he was going, some big-wig preachers started demanding a sign from heaven to test him. ¹²Jesus shook his head in bewilderment and wondered, "Why are y'all always looking for proof? I'm telling y'all right now that no sign will be given to you." ¹³He saddled right back up and rode back the way he'd come.

¹⁴As they were on the trail, they had forgotten to get some provisions and just had one little old loaf of bread. ¹⁵Jesus used it as an illustration and said, "Y'all be careful. Beware of the yeast that infiltrates the bread of Herod and all them big-wig preachers."

¹⁶With that being said, they began to argue about whether or not to eat the bread they had. Jesus shook his head, amazed that they couldn't understand something as simple as what he'd said. ¹⁷So he asked 'em, "Why are you squabblin' over bread? Have any of you been paying attention to what's happened? ¹⁸You have eyes don't you? You have ears don't you? ¹⁹Did any of you see what happened when I fed the five thousand with five loaves? How many baskets of leftovers did y'all pick up?"

"Twelve," they said.

²⁰"And when I fed the four thousand with seven tortillas, how many baskets of leftovers did you pick up then?"

"Seven."

²¹"Do you still not see and get it?" Jesus asked.

²²When they finally reached Bethsaida, a blind man was brought to Jesus for healing. ²³He led the man outside the town, and after spitting in the guy's eyes, Jesus placed his hands on the man's eyes and asked, "What do you see?"

²⁴The fellow said, "I see people, but they look like walking bushes."

²⁵Jesus placed his hands on the man's eyes again. When the man opened his eyes again, he saw everything the way he should. ²⁶Jesus sent him home, but told him not to go back to town.

²⁷Jesus and his cowboys rode off towards Caesarea Philippi. While they were riding along, Jesus asked, "What's the word on the street about me?"

²⁸They said, "Some say John the Baptist reborn and others call you Elijah, or some other Cowboy of God from the old days."

²⁹Jesus continued to look ahead and said, "Who do y'all think I am?"

Pete spat his words quickly, "You are the Chosen One. The one God said he'd send to save us all."

³⁰After a long silence, Jesus said, "Don't tell anyone else…

not yet."

³¹Then Jesus told 'em about all the things that the Son of Man would go through. He told 'em about all the suffering and rejection he would face from the religious know-it-alls, big-wig preachers, and others. He told 'em flat out that he would die and three days later he would be raised from the dead.

³²During this conversation, Pete took Jesus aside and tried to scold him about talking about such foolish things.

³³Jesus wasn't having none of it and said loud enough for everyone to hear, "Get back satan before I stomp a mud hole in ya. You're only looking at things from a man's perspective and not the ways of God."

³⁴About this time, there were a bunch of people around. Jesus stood up in his stirrups and let out a whistle for everyone to pay attention. ³⁵He told 'em all, "If anyone wants to ride for my outfit, he's gotta give up always looking out for himself. You've got be ready for the world to make fun of you. Be ready to saddle up with me every single day. Any cowboy that rides for himself will end up dead, but anyone who rides only for me and the Good News will find true life. ³⁶What good does owning the whole world do for a cowboy without a soul? ³⁷What kind of man would trade his soul for a two dollar lie? ³⁸If any cowboy is ashamed to ride with me down here, that fellow won't find himself riding in the green

Gospel of Mark 33

pastures of heaven with the Boss and his angels."

Chapter 9

Jesus kept on a talkin', "There are some cowboys who are right here that will not die before they see the awesome display of God's Outfit."

²Six days later, Jesus took along Pete, James, and John. They rode up on a high mountain to be alone. As they were sitting there, Jesus' appearance transformed before their very eyes. ³His clothes became so white it almost blinded 'em. ⁴Then the great cowboys of old, Elijah and Moses, walked up and started talking to Jesus.

⁵Pete jumped up quickly and said, "Hey boss! What do you think about us making a memorial about this day. I could make one for you, one for Elijah, and one for old Moses." ⁶Pete only said this because when he got scared, he usually just ran-off at the mouth. But he wasn't the only one who was scared of what they were seeing.

⁷Then a cloud seemed to pass over them all and a voice came from it saying, "This is my boy, the Son that I love. When he says something, you'd all best listen."

⁸And as quick as that, everyone looked around and Elijah and Moses were gone. Only Jesus and his three cowboys were left.

⁹As they rode back down, Jesus told 'em not to tell anyone

about what they'd seen until he'd been killed and had come back from the dead. ¹⁰The three cowboys agreed, but from time to time they asked each other what they thought he meant by, "...come back from the dead."

¹¹The three cowboys questioned Jesus by asking him, "Why do the religious experts say that Elijah has to come first?"

¹²He said, "Elijah does come first. He brings everything back and gets everything ready for the Chosen One. ¹³They treated Elijah poorly and they'll do the same to the Chosen One, who will, according to the Word of God, be treated even worse."

¹⁴When they rounded a small hill and trotted up to where the rest of cowboys were, they heard a bunch of people squabblin'. ¹⁵As soon as they spotted Jesus, they ran to say hello to him.

¹⁶"What's all the bickerin' about?" Jesus asked while he swung off his horse.

¹⁷One of the men from the crowd spoke up quickly. "Jesus, I brought my son to be healed by you. He is possessed by an evil spirit that keeps him from talking and every once in a while, ¹⁸it throws my boy to the ground. It scares the tar out of me because he starts a foamin' at the mouth while gnashing his teeth like a wild hog. He then becomes as rigid

as a felled lodgepole pine. I asked your cowboys for help, but they was useless."

[19] Jesus told all of them, "Do I have to do everything myself? What're y'all gonna do when I'm gone? Bring the boy over here."

[20] They brought the boy over and when the devil inside him saw Jesus, it threw the boy on the ground in a violent seizure. The boy was foaming and frothing at the mouth like a rabid coyote.

[21] "How long has this been going on?" Jesus asked.

The father replied, [22] "Since he was just knee-high, this devil has been throwing my poor son in the water and even in the branding fire a time or two trying to kill him. I can't let him out of my sight and I'm wore plum out, sir. Will you help us if you can?"

[23] "What do you mean, 'If I can'?" Jesus raised an eyebrow and asked. "Ain't nothin' impossible for a man that believes."

[24] The man fell to his knees and sobbed, "I want to believe, but you've got to help me!"

[25] Jesus saw that quite a crowd was starting to take notice of what was going on. His words latched onto the evil spirit as he said, "You that is tormenting this boy, I command you to leave and never show your face again."

²⁶The demon caused the boy to be thrown to the ground one last time as it did as Jesus commanded and high-tailed it out of there. The boy lay there still on the ground and many folks started murmuring that he was dead. ²⁷But Jesus reached down and took hold of the boys hand and he stood up.

²⁸Later, when Jesus was alone with his cowboys, they asked him, "Why couldn't we get rid of that demon?"

²⁹Jesus said, "Prayer is the only thing that will whip those kind."

³⁰Leaving that part of the country, Jesus and his cowboys rode through the area known as Galilee, but he didn't want anyone to know he was there. Jesus wanted as much time alone with his cowboys as he could so he could ³¹teach 'em all they would need to know. He told them, "God's Top Hand is going to be double-crossed and handed over to his enemies. They're going to kill him, but he's going to come back from the dead three days later." ³²None of his cowboys really knew what he was talking about and they were too chicken to ask him.

³³They arrived at Capernaum one evening and as they settled in for the night, Jesus asked his cowboys what they had been discussing on the ride over. ³⁴None of 'em wanted to say anything because they had all been arguing about which of 'em was the best hand.

³⁵He told 'em all to gather 'round, for he had known all along what they had been saying. Jesus said, "Whoever wants to be the top hand in my outfit has to be willing to ride drag and let everyone else go in front of him."

³⁶He called a little kid over to him that had been playing nearby. He put the little one on his knee and said, ³⁷"Whoever is willing to care for the little ones of this world is the one who rides for me...more importantly, he rides for my Dad."

³⁸John piped up and said, "Boss, we saw a guy just the other day that was getting rid of evil spirits by using your name. We stopped him because he didn't ride with us."

³⁹Jesus put a stop to that foolishness at once, "Why'd you stop him? Ain't no one can use my name for good things and then in the next breath say something bad about me. ⁴⁰If someone ain't riding against us, then they are riding for us. ⁴¹Even a person that gives you a drink from their canteen because you ride for God's Top Hand will be rewarded for it. ⁴²But here's a warning and you better listen close: If anyone causes one of these little ones to abandon their faith and follow the outlaw's trail, well, it would be better for that cowboy if he was tied to an anvil and thrown in the ocean. ⁴³If your hand causes you to sin, then you'd be better off by chopping it off. It'd be better to have one hand in life than both hands in hell. Same way with your feet. ⁴⁵If one of your feet takes you someplace you ought not be, it'd be better for

Gospel of Mark

you to cut it off than to walk all high and mighty right into hell. ⁴⁷If your eye keeps looking at things it shouldn't, tear that sucker right out. It's better to ride for God's Outfit with a patch over one eye than to see what hell is like with both. ⁴⁸⁻⁵⁰Here's the skinny of it: Everyone will go through a test of fire; will you be refined by it or destroyed by it? My way will refine you and bring you peace. The other way? Not so much."

Chapter 10

Then Jesus left and rode off to the region along Jordan Creek. Once again, the crowds of people found him and he taught them about riding for God's Outfit.

²Some of the big-wig preachers showed their ugly hides and tried to throw a heel trap at him and get him to say something wrong. They asked him, "Is it right for a cowboy to divorce his wife?"

³Jesus turned it back on 'em and said, "What did Moses have to say about it?"

⁴They puffed out their chests as they began to show off their scripture knowledge. "Moses said it was fine. All a cowboy has to do is give her a paper that says they are divorced."

⁵But Jesus was already shaking his head. "Yeah, he said that, but only because you are weak and don't understand nothin'. ⁶From the beginning, God made cowboys and cowgirls. ⁷It's because of this that a cowboy will leave his own parents and unite with a cowgirl and the ⁸two will become one. In God's eyes, they are one person. ⁹And what God has joined together, what right has anyone else to come and try to sort off one?"

¹⁰Later on in the house, the cowboys asked Jesus about

what he'd said. ¹¹⁻¹²He told them, "Anyone (cowboy or cowgirl) who divorces and marries someone else commits adultery. It's as plain and simple as that."

¹³In those days, people were always bringing their kids to see Jesus so he could bless 'em. It happened so frequently that they cowboys started trying to keep people from doing it. ¹⁴But when Jesus saw what was happening he put a stop to it. He said, "Let them kiddos come to me. God's Outfit belongs to kiddos like these. ¹⁵I'm telling you straight that anyone who doesn't come to me with the faith and honesty of a little kid has no place on my Dad's ranch." ¹⁶Jesus blessed every kid that ever came to see him.

¹⁷As Jesus rode out one day on his way to Jerusalem, a fellow come running up and got down on his knees in front of him. As he was hunkered over he asked, "Excuse me good cowboy, but what must I do to live forever?"

¹⁸Jesus pulled up and asked, "Why do you call me good? No one is good except God himself. Besides that, ¹⁹you know what the codes say, 'Don't kill. Don't jack with another man's jenny. Don't take what ain't yours. Don't say things about others that you know ain't right. Don't talk ill of another man, and hold your mom and dad in high regard.'"

²⁰The man was smilin' and pattin' himself on the back on the back so hard Jesus was afraid he'd hurt himself. The guy said, "Well I'm as good as gold then. I've done all these

things since I was just a little nub."

²¹As Jesus was looking at him, he felt a tremendous love for the man and so he told him the truth of the matter. "Hang on there cowboy. One more thing: Go and sell every single thing you own and give it to the poor and you will be a rich man in heaven. Once you're done selling, then come and ride for me and I'll take care of you."

²²You would have thought that Jesus had just shot the man's favorite dog. The man was wealthy and he wasn't about to sell everything he had and put his life in the hands of someone else, let alone God.

²³As the man walked away with his tail between his legs, Jesus told his cowboys, "A man who won't let go of the world will never be able to fit through the entrance to God's place."

²⁴The cowboys all looked at each other in bewilderment at what Jesus had just said. Jesus continued, "I tell you the truth, ²⁵it'd be easier for a bull to jump through a cinch ring than for a rich man to fit through the gate into heaven."

²⁶They all started talking at once, but the questions were the same. "Then who can fit through?"

²⁷Jesus turned to them and said, "A cowboy that thinks he can get there on his own will never make it, but a cowboy who trusts in God and God alone will never miss the gate... or anything else."

Gospel of Mark

²⁸Pete spoke up and said, "Well, we've left everything behind to ride with you."

²⁹Jesus nodded and added, "Listen, there ain't a cowboy alive who has left their home, their job, their family, or anything or anyone, in order to ride with me ³⁰that won't get a hundred times back anything they think they've left. It won't be easy, but it'll all be worth it. But one thing to remember: ³¹Those that ride the longest will be the last to ride through the gate. A good cowboy always makes sure everyone is through the gate before he gets off and shuts it."

³²They were still riding for Jerusalem, with Jesus in the lead. The cowboys weren't sure of what was coming so Jesus pulled them aside and told 'em what they should expect. ³³"This will be the end of the line for me, boys. I'm going to be double-crossed by a pard and the religious institution that claims to serve God. They are going to sentence me to death and hand me over to the Romans. ³⁴These people are going to mock me, spit on me, beat me nearly to death, and ultimately kill me. Yet all of this is supposed to happen, because I'm going to come back from the dead three days later."

³⁵The brothers, James and John, took Jesus to one side and said, "We'd like for you to do us a favor."

³⁶"What is it that you want?"

³⁷They looked at each other and continued, "When you

take your spot at the head of the ranch, we want to ride on your right and left. You know, up front with you."

³⁸But Jesus said, "You don't have any idea what you're asking for. Do you think you will be able to ride the trail that I'm fixing to go down?"

³⁹"Yes sir!" They exclaimed.

Then he said to them, "Well, in that case, you will travel down the same trail as I do, ⁴⁰but it ain't for me to decide who rides to my left and my right. These spots are reserved for who my Dad wants there."

⁴¹Now the other cowboys heard what was happening and they got all frazzled up over the conversation. ⁴²Jesus told 'em all to quiet down and listen to what he had to say. "This outfit don't work the way it does everywhere else. Everyone down here wants titles and positions so they can tell others what to do and be looked up to like they are something special. ⁴³But here in this outfit, it works completely opposite. ⁴⁴The top hand among you will be the one who puts everyone else first and himself last. ⁴⁵For even the Greatest Top Hand did not come down here to ride all high and mighty, but he came to serve others, and to offer his life as a ransom for everyone else."

⁴⁶They were passing through Jericho and on the outskirts they ran into a blind beggar named, Bartimaeus. He was

Gospel of Mark

sitting beside the road. ⁴⁷When the blind fellow heard that it was Jesus riding by, he hollered out, "Jesus! Please help me!" ⁴⁸A lot of people tried to shut him up because of the racket he was making, but he kept it up. "Jesus, please, please help me!"

⁴⁹Jesus reined up and said, "Tell him to come here."

People around him said, "Quick, get up. Jesus is calling you. Don't be scared!" Immediately, like a shot from a gun, ⁵⁰he threw off his poncho, jumped up, and ran in the direction of Jesus.

⁵¹Jesus said to him as he got close, "What do you want from me?"

The fellow slid to a stop and said, "Please let me see again."

⁵²Jesus smiled and said, "Go, your faith has given you back your eyes."

And just like that, the man's sight returned, but he didn't leave…he followed Jesus.

Chapter 11

They slowed to a walk as they got close to Jerusalem. Jesus sent two of his cowboys ahead to a little cow camp and ²told them, "When you get there, you will find an unbroke colt tied to the fence. ³If anyone questions you, just tell them that the Lord needs it and will return it shortly."

⁴They found the colt and sure enough, ⁵some people started asking them where they were taking it. ⁶The cowboys told them that Jesus needed it and the people said nothing more and let them pass. ⁷They brought the colt to Jesus and they threw their coats on its back as saddle blankets and then Jesus hopped up there. ⁸Then Jesus started his ride into Jerusalem and people honored him by throwing their own coats on the ground so that even the colt's feet that carried him wouldn't touch the dirt. Some people even cut branches off of nearby trees and laid them down in the road for Jesus' mount to walk on.

⁹This was quite a sight to see and people in front of Jesus and behind him were shouting,

> "The Lord will save us! Here's to the One who rides in the name of the Lord! ¹⁰Here's to the coming of the outfit that our father David talked so much about. Here! Here!"

¹¹Jesus rode straight to the main church in town to talk to

his Daddy in heaven. After he was done, he went out to the little town of Bethany with his twelve cowboys.

¹²The next morning they got up and rode out of Bethany. Jesus was hungry and ¹³he saw a fig tree a little ways off the trail. The tree was bright and full of life and leaves, but there were no figs, despite that it was a little early in the season. Jesus rode off from the tree and ¹⁴said loud enough for his cowboys to hear, "May you never make fruit again."

¹⁵When they got to Jerusalem, they went straight to the main church area of town. Jesus jumped off his horse and started throwing the tables across the courtyard of those people who were selling animals for sacrifices. He made quite an impression in the way he handled the money changer's booths. ¹⁶It had become more of a carnival than a place to worship God. ¹⁷He jumped up on a stone and shouted for all to hear, "Everyone listen! Didn't God's writings say:

'My house will be called a house of prayer for the whole world'?

But you all here have turned it into a circus and a robber's roost!"

¹⁸When Jesus finished speaking the truth, some religious experts and big-wig preachers immediately started trying to figure out how they could kill this cowboy.

[19] Jesus and his cowboys spent all day in town. They left as the sun started to set and they loped off into the darkness.

[20] The next morning, they took the same route as the day before. They passed by that fig tree and many of them noticed it was dead. [21] Pete said, "Look Boss, the fig tree you cursed is dead."

[22] Jesus didn't so much as turn his head as he said, "Have faith in God. [23] This here's the truth: If someone tells a mountain to go jump in the sea, and he does not doubt that God can do it, but believes in the power of God wholeheartedly, then it will happen. [24] This is why I keep telling y'all that when you pray, believe in your hearts that God hears you and has already done what you asked. [25] But don't let anything get in the way of your prayers. If you are holding a grudge or have not done something that someone else asked you for, then go do that so that your Boss in heaven will do the same for you."

[27] They rode in Jerusalem again and headed straight for the main church area. While Jesus was walking amongst the people, some of the big-wigs that ran the place came up to him and asked him, [28] "So just who do you think you are, hotshot? Who gave you the right to come in here like you own this joint?"

[29] Jesus turned to them nonchalantly and said, "I'll answer you if you answer me. [30] Did John's authority to baptize come

from heaven or did he just make it up on his own? Answer that."

³¹The huddled together like squabblin' birds at a bird bath. "If we say it was from heaven, he'll ask us why didn't we believe in what John was doing. ³²But if we say it was just his own idea, all these people will get mad because they believe that John was a true cowboy of God."

³³Finally, they turned back to Jesus and said, "We don't know."

Jesus shook his head and then said, "If you don't even know who John was, then I ain't going to tell you who I am or where my authority comes from."

Chapter 12

Then Jesus gathered everyone that wanted to learn around him. He taught them with stories they could understand and relate to: "A man started a ranch and strung all the wire and set every post. He even built a big nice entrance with a gate. After that, he leased the ranch on shares to some cowboys who wanted to get started in the business. The rancher moved away to another part of the country, but at the time of shipping calves, ²he sent one of his cowboys back to get the share of his calves for the lease. ³But the cowboys on the ranch grabbed the cowboy and beat the crap out of him and sent him back without a single calf. ⁴The rancher sent another hand over there to get his share of the calves and they beat that fellow also and sent him back empty handed. ⁵The next cowboy the rancher sent was even killed. Still, the rancher sent hand after hand to get what was owed and right. They beat or killed every single one. ⁶Finally, the rancher was all out of hands and the only one left to send was his only son—the son he loved more than anything else. The rancher finally sent him, thinking, 'Surely they will respect my son.' But the evil cowboys saw the son coming and ⁷said to one another, 'Look, the rancher sends his own son. If we kill him, then the rancher will have no one to leave his ranch to and we will have the boy's inheritance.' ⁸So they ambushed the rancher's grown son, killed him, and then left his body right outside the front gate."

⁹Jesus continued the story, "So what do y'all think the rancher will do? He will come back himself and kill those no-account rustlers and give the ranch to other cowboys that will be thankful for the opportunity to ride for him. ¹⁰Have you not read God's words that say:

>'The calf the cowboys culled has now become the sire bull. ¹¹This is from God and everyone that sees it is amazed?'"

¹²Now this really got them big-wig preacher's feathers ruffled. They wanted to arrest him, but the crowds loved what Jesus was teaching. The big-wigs knew he had just told this story about them, but they just skulked away to scheme against him.

¹³Then the big-wigs sent some slick-willy politicians, along with some silver-tongued preachers, in an attempt to trap Jesus and make him look bad. ¹⁴They strolled up to Jesus like they were all friends and said, "Hey there professor, we know you are a straight shooter and don't say things just so people will like you. We know you teach the truth straight from God, but we've got a question for ya: ¹⁵Should those of us who follow God really be paying taxes to Caesar?"

But Jesus saw right through their underhanded scheme and said, "Do you think I'm going to fall for your silly games? Bring me one of these coins you use to pay your taxes and let me see it." ¹⁶One of them pulled a coin out of his pocket and flipped it to Jesus. He held the coin up and asked, "Who's picture is on this coin?"

"Caesar's," they answered.

[17]Jesus nodded his head in agreement and said, "Give Caesar the things that belong to Caesar and give God the things that belong to God." And he tossed the coin back.

Everyone who heard him was amazed.

[18]Some Sadducees (religious politicians who didn't believe in life after death—meaning they tried to get as much out of this life as they could) took their turn trying to trap Jesus. [19]They asked him, "Sir, Moses told us that God said, 'If a man's brother is married and dies, then the brother is to marry his former sister-in-law and have some kids in memory of his dead brother.' But what about this scenario? [20]Say there were seven brothers and the oldest brother marries a woman, but dies before they have any kids. [21]Then the next brother marries her and he dies before they have any kids. [22]This goes on until every brother has married her and died without a single kid being born. Finally, the woman dies too. [23]If there is life after death, whose wife will she be in heaven?"

[24]Jesus said to them, "Y'all ain't got a clue what you're talking about. Y'all don't know God's words from a cow turd. And you certainly don't know anything about the

power of God. ²⁵When people are raised from the dead and enter heaven, none of them will be married to anyone, but rather, they will be like the angels. ²⁶But, let's cut to the chase here. Y'all are asking me about life after death and you don't even believe in that. Have you not read in Moses' book, in the section about the burning bush, how God said to him, 'I am the God of Abraham, the God of Isaac, and the God of Jacob'? He didn't say he had been the God of those great guys, but that he is the God of them. ²⁷Those guys are alive with him because he is the God of the living, not the dead. You boys couldn't find a forty pound truth if it was hanging off the end of your nose."

²⁸A religious lawyer had walked up during this debate and was impressed with Jesus' answer. He asked Jesus a question of his own. "Which commandment is the most important one of 'em all?"

²⁹Jesus turned to him and said, "I'll tell you which one is most important: It's from one of Moses' books, 'Listen up, Israel. Our God is the only God there is. ³⁰You must ride for God with all your heart, soul, and mind. You've got to ride for him with everything ounce of strength you've got.' ³¹But there is another commandment that is just as important as this one. 'Care as much about the well-being of others as much as you care about the well-being of yourself.' These two things are more important than all the offerings and sacrifices a person could ever make."

³²"Well said, sir," the lawyer replied. "You speak the truth in that there is one, and only one, God. ³³To ride for him with all your heart, all your soul, and all your strength, and to love your neighbor as much as you love yourself is more important than all the sacrifices in the world."

³⁴Jesus saw that the light was starting to come on for this fellow, so he told him, "You are not far from God's Outfit right now." After that, no one dared ask any more questions trying to trap him.

³⁵Later on, Jesus was giving a clinic at the main church in town about how to ride for God. He asked them, "Why do those that stress religious rules claim that God's Top Hand will be a son of the great King David? ³⁶I ask this because even David, in his book, said,

"'God told my Boss, Ride to my right and watch as I trample over all of your enemies and you ride right over them.'"

³⁷Since David himself called God's Top Hand his 'Boss,' how then can the Chosen One be his son?"

People shook their heads in wonderful amazement at the things that Jesus taught.

³⁸He also taught them: "Keep a sharp lookout for those that teach religious rules! They like to ride around with their fancy tack and hand-tooled saddles. ³⁹They like it when

Gospel of Mark

people look up to them like they are all high and mighty. ⁴⁰But these fellows would cheat a widow out of her last piece of bread and then go and make a long, eloquent prayer at a public gathering. Because they act like this, they will be punished severely."

⁴¹Jesus rested between his clinics and sat near the offering box in church. He watched as people gave their offering. Many rich people put in a big wad of cash, ⁴²but then a poor widow came and dropped in two small coins.

⁴³Jesus immediately got all his cowboy's attention and said, "Did y'all see that? I tell you the truth, that poor lady right there has given more than all the others combined. ⁴⁴They gave a little bit of their riches, but she gave everything she had to live on."

Chapter 13

As Jesus and his cowboys were leaving the church that day, one of 'em said, "Hey Boss, look at how big and pretty this building is. Isn't it impressive?"

²Jesus replied, "You got that right. All these buildings are impressive, but not a single one will be left standing. They will all be knocked down."

³Later that day, Jesus sat on Olive Hill, across from the main church. Peter, James, John, and Andy came to him and asked, ⁴"When will all this stuff you've been talking about happen? Will you give us a whistle, or will there be a signal that the end of time is going to kick off?"

⁵Jesus was adamant when he said, "Don't let anyone pull the wool over your eyes. ⁶There will be many people claiming to be me, and a lot of people will believe them. ⁷There will be wars and threats of wars, but y'all don't have to be afraid. Sure, these things will happen, but just because they happen doesn't mean that the end is right around the corner. ⁸Nations will go to war against other nations and there will be fighting all over the world. There will be earthquakes, and droughts, and people will starve, but these things are just the first sharp pain of the birth that will come later."

⁹"When you see these things start to happen, be careful, but be ready also. You will be arrested in the towns and beat-

en right inside the churches. You will stand trial because you ride for me. This may sound bad, but it is a great opportunity for you to tell others about the free gift I give everyone who rides for me. ¹⁰The Good News about what I will do must be spread to everyone in the world. ¹¹But don't go to worrying about what you will say before you are arrested. When that time comes, God will put the right words in your mouth and the courage in your heart. It won't be you that is talking, it will be the Holy Spirit."

¹²Jesus continued, "It's going to get so bad in the end that people will turn against the ones they love the most. They'll turn in their brothers, their kids, their parents, and anyone else for a little reward and these people will be killed because they ride for me. ¹³If you ride for me, people are going to hate you and want you dead. But the cowboy that rides all the way to the end for me will be saved."

¹⁴"Be ready to high-tail it for the hills when you see the anti-christ at the altar of the church. ¹⁵When you see that, you don't even stop to put something in your saddlebags, you just jump on and go. ¹⁶If you are gathering cattle and see it, don't go back for a change of clothes, just whip and spur out of there! ¹⁷It'll be a real bad time for those that are nursing children. ¹⁸Just pray that this hard time don't come in the winter when times are at their hardest. ¹⁹I'm telling y'all, these times will be harder than any other time in history. ²⁰In fact, the times will be so hard that unless God inter-

venes, and he will, not a single follower of mine will survive. But for the sake of those who ride for me, God will step in and help."

²¹"So if you see anyone that says, 'Look! There is Jesus,' or another says, 'I heard Jesus came back,' don't believe them. ²²There will be many counterfeits that will come and do things that will amaze people. Some that ride for me will be deceived, too. ²³So y'all better watch out. I'm giving you a heads up about these things ahead of time."

²⁴"In the days that follow these hard times,

'The sun will go out and the moon will lose its light; ²⁵the stars will fall from the skies and the great power in universe will be shaken.'

²⁶"Then everyone will see the Top Hand riding through the clouds with a power so awesome that it will be undeniable. ²⁷God's Chosen One, His Son, the Top Hand, will send his angels out to gather all his cowboys and cowgirls that ride for his brand and gather them together from the furthest parts of the earth all the way to heaven. Not one will be left behind."

²⁸The cowboys sat in awe as he continued, "Learn a lesson from a simple tree. When the leaves start to bud out, you know that spring has arrived and summer is near. ²⁹In the same way, when you see all these things happening, you

know that the Top Hand is riding out of the gate and coming for you. ³⁰I'm telling you the truth when I say that those who ride for me during that time, not all of them will die before all of this I've told you about happens. ³¹The current heaven and the earth you see now will end, but my words will never prove untrue."

³²Jesus held up a cautionary hand, "But no one, and I mean no one—not the angels in heaven, or myself—knows when the exact time will take place. Only God knows. ³³So keep a sharp lookout and whatever you do, be ready! I can't express enough the need to be ready to ride because you will not know when the time will come. ³⁴It's kind of like the wagon boss leaving the ranch and telling each of the cowboys what jobs they are supposed to do while he is gone. He even puts one cowboy at the gate to watch for his return. ³⁵I'm posting y'all at the gate to watch. You don't know if the wagon boss is coming back in the evening, or at noon, or before the rooster crows. ³⁶You don't want to be caught napping when he arrives. ³⁷Stay alert and watch like I've told you to do."

Chapter 14

Two days before the Passover and the feast of the Flat Bread, the big-wig preachers and religious lawmakers were trying to figure out a way to have Jesus killed. They all agreed that they would have to do it before the feast, and ²before the special Passover celebration, because they didn't want the people to riot.

³While Jesus was staying in Bethany at the house of a fellow named Simon (who had a terrible skin disease), he relaxed at the table. A woman came by the house and had a small, but extremely expensive jar of aromatic oil. She opened it and poured the whole thing on Jesus' head (this was a great honor she was trying to give him).

⁴But some of the people who were there took offense at the gesture. They said, "Why waste such an expensive gift on one person? ⁵That could have been sold for three hundred silver pieces and the money could have taken care of many poor people!" Then they all started giving the woman a hard time and scolding her.

⁶But Jesus shut them up right quick. "Y'all leave her alone. She hasn't done anything to you, but she has done something extremely nice for me. ⁷You will always have the poor to help, but you will not always have me around. She tried to do something special for me and I appreciate it. ⁸She has

prepared my body for burial before I'm even dead. ⁹When my story is told; when the Good News is preached all over the world; the story of what she did here today will be told in honor of what she did."

¹⁰While this was going on, Judas Iscariot, one of Jesus' cowboys, rode off to meet with the big-wig preachers and religious lawmakers for the sole purpose of double-crossing his boss. ¹¹The scoundrels he talked to were tickled pink at the information Judas gave them about Jesus and they promised to reward him handsomely. They all concocted a plan to betray and capture Jesus.

¹²On the first day of the Flat Bread feast is when the Passover lamb is sacrificed. Jesus' cowboys asked him where he wanted to eat the Passover meal. ¹³He sent a couple of his cowboys to the city and ¹⁴said, "When you get into town, you'll see a man carrying a canteen. Follow him. When he goes into a house, knock on the door and tell the owner, 'The Boss asks, Which room shall I stay in and eat the Passover meal with my cowboys?' ¹⁵He will immediately take you upstairs to a large furnished room. Get everything started and the rest of us will be along shortly."

¹⁶The cowboys rode off and found everything just like Jesus said they would. After it happened just like he said it would, they went upstairs and started cooking.

¹⁷When evening arrived, Jesus arrived at the house with

the rest of his men, including Judas the Betrayer. ¹⁸While they were eating, Jesus commented, "One of you eating here with me is a double-crosser."

¹⁹You could have heard a pin drop and then one by one, each cowboy said, "It's not me, Boss!"

²⁰Jesus had just sat a bowl down that he had passed around and everyone had dipped their bread into. He said, "The double-crosser has just dipped his hand in the same bowl as I did. ²¹He will betray me because God said it would happen, but it would be better for the double-crossing cur dog if he'd never been born."

²²While they were eating, he took some bread, gave thanks to God for it, and shared pieces of it with all his cowboys. After handing some to everyone, he said, "This bread is for y'all and it represents my body that I also give for y'all."

²³He then took his cup, and after giving thanks to God for what was inside it, he shared a little with everyone else. They all drank it and he said, ²⁴"This is my blood. My blood is the seal on God's new promise. A promise, by my blood that will be shed, for the many. ²⁵I won't drink another drop of wine until the day when I drink it in my Daddy's place."

²⁶They all gathered around and sang a few songs and then they struck a long trot for Olive Hill.

When they got there, ²⁷Jesus said to them, "It's fixing to

get real bad, my friends. It was written about long ago when it said,

> 'God will strike down the Top Hand, and his herd will be scattered.'

²⁸But after I come riding back from the grave, I will meet you in Galilee."

²⁹Pete spoke up quickly and said, "All these boys may run off and leave you, but I won't."

³⁰Jesus replied kindly, "Listen Pete. Today—actually, this very night—before the rooster crows in the morning, you will deny you even know me. Not just once, but three times."

³¹Pete shook his head and argued, "Boss, even if I have to die with you, I would never say that I didn't know you."

All the other cowboys agreed and said the same thing.

³²They all saddled up and rode off towards Gethsemane. When they got there, he told all the cowboys to wait there and pray. ³³He motioned for Pete, James, and John to follow him. Jesus looked worse than they'd ever seen him and ³⁴he told them, "I want y'all to stay here with me. I'm so full of dread that my heart feels like it is going to stop. Please keep me company. I need y'all right now, pards."

³⁵Jesus went far enough as to be out of sight and fell down

to his knees. He looked up to heaven and said, ³⁶"Dad, you can find another way—can't you? It doesn't have to happen like this does it? I sure don't want to drink from this cup of agony that sits before me."

After a moment's pause, he continued, "But you know what, Dad? It's not about what I want. It's about what you want."

³⁷He got up and went back to where he'd left Pete, James, and John. They were all sound asleep. He woke Pete up and said, "Did you really fall asleep at a time like this? ³⁸Keep a sharp lookout. Start praying so that you will not be ambushed by any sinful temptations. I know you want to do what's right, but talk is cheap."

³⁹Jesus went back to his prayer spot for a while and then returned only to find them all asleep again. ⁴⁰They woke up and just kind of sat there, unsure what to say. They knew that they had messed up again.

⁴¹He went away again and came back a third time, only to find them asleep again. He got them up and said, "Y'all rested up now? Enough is enough. The time has come and here is the betrayer bringing the wolves into the sheep's pen. ⁴²Get up, boys. It's time to go. Here comes the double-crossing cur dog now.

⁴³Just as the words came out of Jesus' mouth, Judas arrived

with a crowd of people. Among them were soldiers, religious lawmakers, and big-wig preachers. ⁴⁴Judas had told them that he would go up kiss Jesus on the cheek. That way they would know who to grab.

⁴⁵Judas sure enough walked right up to Jesus, just like they were good pards, and gave him a kiss on the cheek. ⁴⁶The crowd rushed in and grabbed Jesus.

⁴⁷Just then, one of Jesus' crew pulled out his castrating blade and took a swing at the main preacher's right-hand man, cutting off his ear.

⁴⁸Jesus spoke above the calamity and said, "Am I some vicious outlaw that you come with swords and clubs to arrest me? Why didn't you just take me while I taught in church? ⁴⁹I was right there every day and all of you listened to me. But never mind, these things are happening because my Dad said they would."

⁵⁰When they took Jesus away, all his cowboys high-tailed it out of there, in fear for their lives. ⁵¹One of the cowboys with Jesus was only dressed in overalls. When the mob tried to take him too, ⁵²he slipped out of the overalls that they had a hold of and ran away buck naked.

⁵³They took Jesus to the main preacher's house where a bunch of the people that had plotted against him were gathered. ⁵⁴Pete had circled around and followed them, but

at a safe distance. He snuck into the yard and sat down with some of the night guard and warmed himself by the fire like nothing was going on.

⁵⁵Inside the house, all the people who had the authority to make decisions were trying to find evidence of guilt so they could kill Jesus. ⁵⁶Many people came and made false accusations against him, but they kept contradicting themselves with their testimonies and none of them could be used.

⁵⁷Finally, a few men stood up and lied as they said, ⁵⁸"We heard Jesus say that he would destroy the main church and replace it three days later with one built by God himself." ⁵⁹It sounded good, but they couldn't get their facts straight when questioned.

⁶⁰The main preacher spoke up and asked Jesus, "What do you have to say about all of this? What do you have to say for yourself?"

⁶¹Jesus stood there, silent and stoic.

The preacher then asked, "Are you the Chosen One? Are you the Son of God himself?"

With words that held the power of God, ⁶²Jesus said, "I AM...and you all *should* know it. Soon, you will see me sitting at the right hand of God himself and riding on the clouds of heaven."

Gospel of Mark

⁶³That old preacher started frothing at the mouth when he heard Jesus say this. He said, "Why do we need anything more than the filth he just uttered out of his mouth?! ⁶⁴You all heard his outright lies. What is your verdict?"

They all responded with a guilty verdict and sentenced him to death.

⁶⁵People rushed Jesus and then spit on him. Others blindfolded him and then some took turns sucker-punching him. They sneered and asked, "Hey prophet!? Who hit you? Tell us the truth of what you cannot see."

Then Jesus was led away, all the while people took turns punching and slapping him as he went.

⁶⁶While all this was happening inside, Pete was by the fire trying to stay warm. ⁶⁷One of the preacher's maids happened to walk by and she suddenly pointed at him and said, "I saw you riding with the one they call Jesus!"

⁶⁸Pete looked around like he was shocked. "Who is Jesus? I don't have a clue what you're talking about." He started to walk away as he heard a rooster crow.

⁶⁹The young girl followed him and began telling everyone around her, "He's one of Jesus' cowboys. I saw them riding together."

⁷⁰Pete shook his head and denied everything.

Word spread through the crowd and many started saying, "You're definitely one of the men that rode with Jesus. You've got that 'Galilean Cowboy' look written all over you."

⁷¹Then Pete let out a string of cuss words and he swore in front of everyone, "I do not know this man that y'all are accusing me of riding with. I've never even seen him!"

⁷²The words were no more out of his mouth when Pete heard a rooster crow for the second time. He remembered what Jesus said to him: "Before a rooster crows twice, you will say you don't know me three times."

Pete broke down and cried.

Chapter 15

Very early in the morning, all the religious leaders had made their plan against Jesus. They tied him up and handed him over to Pilate, the local Roman governor in charge.

²Pilate asked Jesus, "Are you the boss of the Jews?"

Jesus replied, "You said it, but I ain't denying it."

³This got the religious leaders all riled up. They were screaming and yelling accusations at Jesus.

⁴Pilate questioned Jesus again, "Are you not going to defend yourself? Listen to everything they are saying about you!"

⁵But Jesus kept his mouth shut and didn't say a word. Pilate was amazed that a man could keep quiet in the face of so many deadly allegations.

⁶During the feast of Flat Bread, and the celebration of Passover, it was a tradition to release one person who was in jail and waiting execution. ⁷There was one particularly nasty fellow named Barabbas, who was locked up for murder.

⁸The crowd asked Pilate to release a prisoner and he asked if they would rather release Jesus or Barabbas. ⁹Pilate said, "Do you want me to let the Boss of the Jews go?" ¹⁰But he knew the religious leaders were just jealous of Jesus. Pilate

was stalling and trying to help him all he could.

¹¹The religious leaders stirred up the crowd against Jesus and they lobbied to have Barabbas released instead.

¹²Pilate, still trying to work out a deal, asked, "Then what am I supposed to do with the one that y'all call the Boss of the Jews?"

¹³They shouted, "String him up on the cross!"

¹⁴Pilate was dismayed and asked, "What has this man done that is so wrong?"

The crowd didn't answer except to chant, "String him up...String him up...String him up!"

¹⁵Pilate didn't want a riot on his hands, so he released Barabbas and sent Jesus to be whipped. After that, he would be strung up on the cross.

¹⁶The Roman soldiers led Jesus into the Governor's mansion and gathered everyone around. ¹⁷They put a purple cape on him and wove a crown of thorns that they smashed on his head. The blood ran into Jesus' eyes and down his face. ¹⁸They paraded mockingly in front of Jesus and saluted him saying, "All hail the Boss of the Jews!"

¹⁹They repeatedly hit him on the head, and spit on Jesus. They knelt down in fake homage and made fun of him for

a long time. ²⁰Finally, when they'd had their fill of fun, they stripped the purple cape off him and led him away to string him up on the cross.

²¹Jesus was carrying the cross piece he would be nailed to, but could go no further due to his injuries. The soldiers grabbed a guy named Simon and made him carry the cross piece.

²²They got up to a hill they call Golgatha (which means "Skull Hill"). ²³They offered him a shot of wine with some numbing stuff mixed in, but Jesus refused it. ²⁴Then they nailed him to the cross and strung him up naked. They gambled and threw dice to see who would get this famous man's clothes. ²⁵This all happened about nine o'clock in the morning.

²⁶They put a sign above Jesus' head that said, "Boss of the Jews" and ²⁷they strung up two outlaws on crosses on both sides of Jesus.

²⁹Many who passed by shouted, "You said you could destroy the church building in three days and then rebuild it…³⁰if you're that powerful, why don't you get yourself off that cross and do it!"

³¹Even the religious leaders made fun of him by saying, "He saved many people, but he can't even save himself. What a joke! ³²If he really is the Chosen One, let him come

down off that cross and we'll believe it."

Even those being crucified with him made fun of him.

33It was now the midday hour, and when the clock had struck high noon, darkness descended over the entire country for three hours. 34About three o'clock int he afternoon, Jesus yelled out, "Eloi, Eloi, lema sabachthani?" which means, "My God, my God, why have you forgotten about me?"

35When some people standing around heard him, they said, "Listen! Jesus is calling out for Elijah!"

36Then someone lifted up a sponge soaked with vinegar and gave it to Jesus. Others said, "Leave him alone. Let's see if Elijah does somehow come riding up to save him."

37Jesus looked up and cried out with a loud voice and let out his last breath. 38In the main church, there was a thick curtain that separated God's holy place from the rest of the building. When Jesus died, this curtain was torn in two from the top to the bottom. No longer would God be separated from his people.

39One of the soldiers who stood at the foot of the cross saw how Jesus died and said, "I think we've screwed up boys. This really was God's Son!"

40Also seeing his death were some women watching from

a distance. These women included Mary Magdalene, Mary the mother of James, and Salome. [41]In Galilee, these women had traveled with Jesus and taken care of him. There were other women there also who had gone to Jerusalem with him.

[42]It was the day before the Day of Rest (the day before the Sabbath Day) and as the sun was setting, [43]a local leader named Joseph of Arimathea and believer of Jesus, went and boldly asked Pilate for the body of Jesus. [44]Pilate seemed surprised to find out that Jesus had already died. [45]He called for a soldier and asked him if Jesus had indeed already died. When it was confirmed, Pilate gave Joseph permission to take the body.

[46]Joseph took a fine linen sheet, took the body down and wrapped it up. He placed Jesus' body in a tomb cut into the rock and rolled a large stone in front of the entrance. [47]Mary Magdalene and Mary, the mother of Joseph, watched the burial happen.

Chapter 16

When the Day of Rest was over, the women brought spices to embalm Jesus' body. ²It was very early on Sunday morning and ³they worried about how they were going to move the heavy stone that had been placed in front of the tomb. ⁴But when they got to the tomb, the stone had already been rolled away.

⁵They walked into the tomb to take care of Jesus' body, but all they saw was a man sitting to the right of where they had laid him. This shocked them and they didn't know what to do or what to say.

⁶But the man said to them, "Whoa! Don't be scared ladies. You are looking for Jesus of Nazareth, but he ain't here. This is where his body was placed, but like I said, he ain't here. ⁷Go tell Jesus' cowboys, especially Pete, that Jesus is heading for Galilee and said to meet him there."

⁸The ladies high-tailed it out of there, not just with a message, but they were scared to death also. They didn't say anything to anyone because they were so afraid.

Note: The following text does not appear in the earliest manuscripts.

⁹After Jesus had been raised from the dead, he first appeared to Mary Magdalene, whom he'd cured of seven

demons. ¹⁰She ended up delivering the message to Jesus' cowboys that he was no longer in the tomb. ¹¹They were still very upset that he had died in the first place and when they heard what she said, they didn't believe a word of it.

¹²Jesus also appeared later to a couple of cowboys that were traveling down the road. ¹³They went and told Jesus' cowboys that they had seen him, but they didn't believe these two either. ¹⁴Finally, Jesus appeared to the eleven remaining cowboys himself. He scolded them for not believing everyone that he had sent to tell them the good news of his coming back from the dead.

¹⁵He told all of 'em, "Y'all get out there and go to every pasture and every place on earth and tell 'em the Good News. Tell 'em that I've opened the gate to God's Outfit and no one ever has to depend on themselves to be perfect, but that I've done it for them. ¹⁶All they have to do is devote their lives to riding for me and be baptized. Everyone who rides for me will get into heaven and those who don't, won't. ¹⁷You'll be able to tell who is a cowboy on my Dad's Outfit because they will drive out demons and speak in languages no one has heard before. ¹⁸They will pick up snakes without being bitten and even have poison given to them without it killing 'em. They will place their hands on people and heal them."

¹⁹After he got done giving them their final instructions, Jesus was whisked up to heaven where he was saddled up at

the right hand of God himself.

[20]The cowboys went and did exactly what Jesus told 'em to and Jesus was right there in spirit working with them. Everything happened just like Jesus said it would because many miraculous signs happened.

Made in the USA
Las Vegas, NV
08 April 2024

88386375R00049